START-A-CRAFT

BEAD WORK

Get started in a new craft with easy-to-follow
projects for beginners

SARA WITHERS

APPLE

A QUINTET BOOK

Published by The Apple Press
6 Blundell Street
London N7 9BH

ISBN 1-84092-099-8

This book was designed and produced by
Quintet Publishing Limited
6 Blundell Street
London N7 9BH

Creative Director: Richard Dewing
Designer: James Lawrence
Project Editor: Diana Steedman
Editor: Lydia Darbyshire
Photographers: Paul Forrester, Colin Bowling

Typeset in Great Britain by
Central Southern Typesetters, Eastbourne
Manufactured in Singapore by Eray Scan Pte Ltd
Printed in China by Leefung-Asco Printers Ltd

CONTENTS

INTRODUCTION

There are those who believe that beads can become an obsession - if so, it is one I can happily recommend. I have worked with beads on a full-time basis for nearly twenty years, and the pleasure I derive from their diversity and their history has increased over the years.

There are few crafts that offer such scope for creativity yet that require so few specialist tools and that do not need a special workshop. All you need are a table, good light, a few tools and some carefully selected beads and findings, and with these you can design and make really exciting pieces of jewellery. You can create something that will attract compliments every time it is worn – or even a piece that will become a family heirloom.

The projects are divided loosely between earrings, necklaces and bracelets, and within each overall group the projects become progressively more difficult. You do not, however, need to begin at the beginning and work through them. If you refer to the techniques section and the instructions for each piece you should be able to make any of them.

The projects use a wide range of techniques and materials in order to extend your skills and offer you opportunities to use your own creative talents. Even if the beads specified for each project are not available from your local supplier, you should be able to use other, similar kinds. For example, we used Guatemalan beads in the Double Stripy Necklace on page 23, and although these beads are readily available in the USA, you may not be able to obtain them in the UK. However, Greek ceramic round beads and tubes are available in the UK, and you could use these instead. All the findings listed for each project should be available in bead shops and most craft shops or by mail order.

Sizes and quantities are difficult to specify. If you are 1.6m (5ft 3in) tall and your friend is 1.7m (5ft 10in) tall, you will not both want to wear the same length of necklace. The quantities specified will allow you to lengthen the projects a little if necessary or to discard some of the smaller beads, if they become dropped or damaged, which will inevitably happen.

The important aspect of these projects is that you should use them to gain an understanding of the basic techniques and to learn how to use the different materials and then quickly begin to apply and adapt them to projects of your own.

If you do become obsessed with beads and want to know more about them, you will find several other books that outline their history and that show some of the potential. You might also want to join a local bead society so that you can share your ideas and experiences with fellow enthusiasts.

But that is for later.

Start with the projects and ideas here and remember, whatever happens, enjoy the beads you use.

MATERIALS AND TECHNIQUES

Before you start to make bead jewellery you need to learn a little about the beads that you can use. You also need to know about the tools, the findings – that is, the necklace fasteners and so on – and the different threads that are available. There is not a lot to learn, but understanding the basics will not only mean that your finished pieces look more professional but will also give you more scope for creativity.

BEADS

Beads are now easier to find and come in a wider range of materials than ever before. Most towns have a craft or haberdashery shop that sells beads, and some larger towns may even have specialist bead shops. You can also obtain a wide variety of beads by mail order, so you should easily be able to make the projects described in this book. Remember, too, that you can also use beads from old or broken necklaces, and, of course, one of the great advantages of bead jewellery is that if you are bored or dissatisfied with a piece, you can simply take it to pieces and use the components to make something quite different.

There are not many technical names for beads, but you should make a note of rocailles and bugles. Both are made of glass: rocailles are small and round, and they range in size from 11/0 (the tiniest) to 6/0 (the largest); bugles are small and tubular. They can usually be bought, by weight, in packets. Although they are often used in bead weaving, loom work and embroidery, they are useful in other designs. Most beads are sold by size, which is quoted in millimetres and which refers to the diameters, not the circumference, of the bead.

When you start to use beads you don't need to know much more about beads than whether you like the shape and colour, but as you become fascinated by them you will want to learn the names of the different kinds and understand the different materials. You will discover a world of Japanese lamp beads, Indian kiln glass beads, Ghanaian powder glass beads and many, many more. This book can introduce you to only a few of the dozens of kinds that are available.

When you buy beads in a shop, always check them for damage. Many beads are made quite roughly, so take care that the ones you are buying are perfect. Make sure that the holes are good and can be easily threaded and, of course, that the colours go well together.

TOOLS

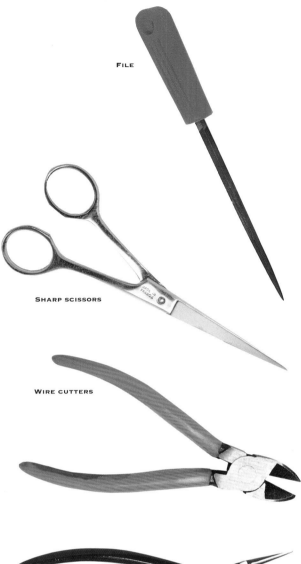

FILE

SHARP SCISSORS

WIRE CUTTERS

ROUND-NOSED PLIERS

FLAT-NOSED PLIERS

You can do a lot with beads with only a few tools. The most essential tool is a pair of round-nosed pliers which you will use, among other things, for making loops for earrings. You need pliers with fairly short, fine points so that you can get close to your work. When you come to make necklaces and use crimps and calottes, you will need some flat-nosed pliers. Sprung round-nosed pliers are also available, and these are excellent for both earring and necklace making. Hold the pliers as shown in the photograph. If you work with beads a lot you should try out different kinds of pliers so that you know which kind you feel most comfortable with. In the projects round-nosed pliers have been specified when they are essential; otherwise the choice is yours.

You will need a pair of sharp scissors for most of the projects, and when you start to work with wire you will need some wire cutters. The sprung wire (see page 9) responds better to heavier wire cutters, but you will be able to cut most wires with quite a light tool. When you work more extensively with wire – the Lapis and Silver Necklace on page 40, for example – you will need a file and a hammer. The file should be fine, and the hammer can be light. As you start to do knotting and beadwork you will need a selection of needles, and you will find a pair of fine-pointed, curved tweezers useful but not essential.

Finally, if you take up loom work you will need a loom. Although the metal looms are not as expensive as the wooden ones, they are not as easy to use. If you become enthusiastic about this technique it will be worth buying a wooden loom.

BEADING NEEDLES

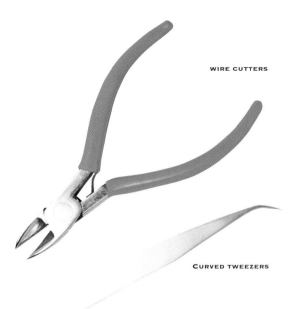

WIRE CUTTERS

CURVED TWEEZERS

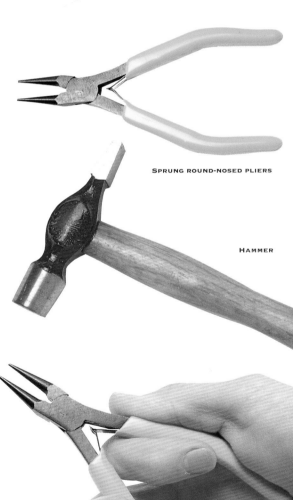

SPRUNG ROUND-NOSED PLIERS

HAMMER

HOLD THE PLIERS LIKE THIS

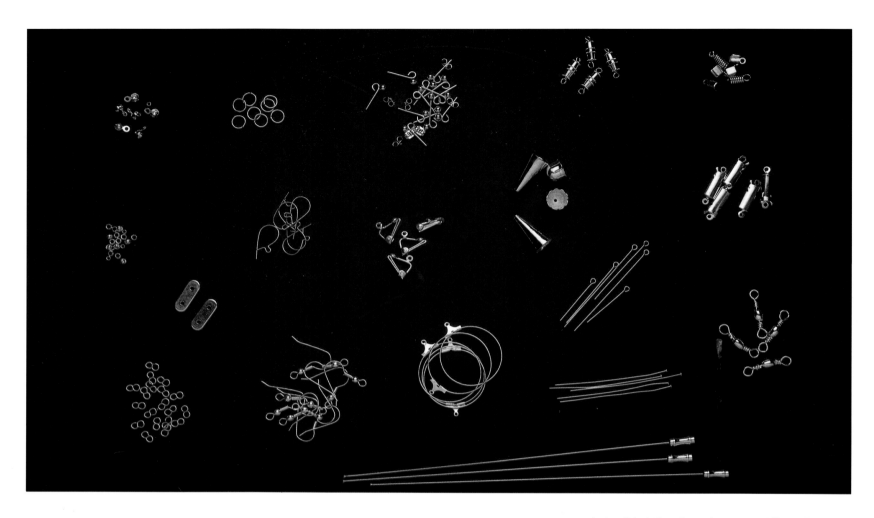

FINDINGS AND THREADS

This is an area in which you need to know some technical terms. All the findings mentioned here are available from many good craft stores, from specialist bead suppliers, and by mail order.

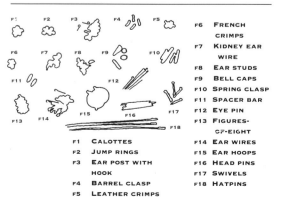

F6	FRENCH CRIMPS	
F7	KIDNEY EAR WIRE	
F8	EAR STUDS	
F9	BELL CAPS	
F10	SPRING CLASP	
F11	SPACER BAR	
F12	EYE PIN	
F13	FIGURES-OF-EIGHT	

F1	CALOTTES	
F2	JUMP RINGS	
F3	EAR POST WITH HOOK	
F4	BARREL CLASP	
F5	LEATHER CRIMPS	
F14	EAR WIRES	
F15	EAR HOOPS	
F16	HEAD PINS	
F17	SWIVELS	
F18	HATPINS	

MAKING EARRINGS

To make straight drop earrings, you will need to put the beads onto an eye pin or a head pin. Eye pins are more versatile than head pins because you can hang other beads from the loops and make longer earrings by adding two together. They are used with their own loop at the bottom of the earring to give a neat finish. If you have large, heavy beads, you can thread them onto 0.8mm or 1.2mm wire or you can use hat pin wires, but you need to clip the ends from the hat pin wires before you use them.

Hoop earrings can be made with 0.8mm wire, as shown on page 10, or from bought hoop findings.

If your ears are not pierced, you will need to use screws or clips, and it is now possible to obtain combined screw/clip findings. All of these are fitted in the same way that we have shown ear wires being fitted. For pierced ears, you will need ear wires, and most of the earrings in the projects in this book have been made with hook or French ear wires. You can, however, also use a post with hook findings, and these are held in place with scrolls or butterflies. Another possibility is kidney wires. You will know from the earrings you have bought and worn in the past which kind of fastening you find most comfortable.

Always buy nickel-free ear wires to avoid allergic reactions. The wires used in the projects shown here are available in sterling silver, and it is well worth the additional expense. Some people can only wear gold, and you can still follow the instructions by simply using gold-colored eye pins, balls and so on, and by buying a few pairs of gold ear wires. You will soon be so adept at making your own jewelry that you will quickly be able to swap the wires from earring to earring.

MAKING NECKLACES AND BRACELETS

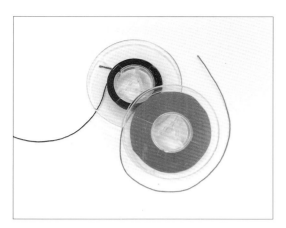

POLYESTER THREAD

When you make a necklace or bracelet you need to know about the different threads and findings that are available.

Simple necklaces and bracelets can be threaded on nylon monofilament, which is available from craft and bead shops and also from fishing equipment shops (you will need to ask for line with a breaking strain of about 6.75kg (15lb). This is best finished with French crimps because it doesn't knot well. Nylon line often shrinks eventually, which makes the necklace or bracelet rather rigid, so it is a good idea to leave about 5mm (¼in) between the last beads and the French crimps.

Tiger tail is nylon-covered steel cable, and it is, as you might expect, ideal for heavy beads. It does not

hang well with light beads, although it is suitable for short necklaces and bracelets. Use it with French crimps and take care that it does not kink as you work.

When you want a necklace that will hang beautifully or when you want to incorporate knotting (see page 33) use either polyester thread or silk thread. These can be finished with French crimps, calottes or knots. There are also some nylon threads on the market, but polyester or silk thread should meet most of your needs. Some colours of polyester thread are available in a waxed form, so you do not always need to use a needle. If you do decide to use this kind of thread with heavy beads, allow the threaded piece to hang for a few days before you finish it because the thread will stretch a little.

Silk thread is strong but delicate, and when you buy it on a card you will find a fine needle attached. The projects using silk thread have been planned to allow you to make the best possible use of your needles.

A fine, strong polyester thread is used with a beading loom.

You will also need a variety of fasteners, depending on the kind of thread you use, if you are sensitive to metals, buy clasps made of sterling silver or gold. The spring clasp, which is used in many of the projects in this book, is efficient and strong. More classic designs might call for screw clasps or bolt rings, which are used with jump rings. Multi-strand necklaces need cones or bell caps.

There are lots of other findings: little figures-of-eight for hanging; spacer bars with two, three or

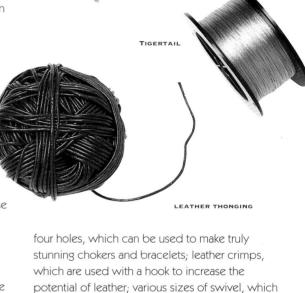

NYLON MONOFILAMENT

TIGERTAIL

LEATHER THONGING

four holes, which can be used to make truly stunning chokers and bracelets; leather crimps, which are used with a hook to increase the potential of leather; various sizes of swivel, which are fun for earrings or chains; and hatpins, which are self-explanatory, but you may have to ask for the clutch on the end separately.

There are also several thicknesses of silver wire, which will be available from the best suppliers. Leather thonging can be bought on a roll or by the metre (yard). Finally, sprung wire is a new idea, which can be bought by weight.

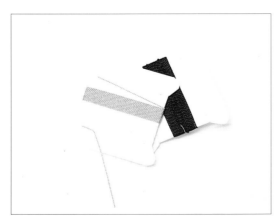

SILK THREAD

SILVER WIRES

SPRUNG WIRES

HOOP EARRINGS

You will need

◊ 0.8mm wire
◊ Black tubing (optional)
◊ 4 small glass beads
◊ 2 large glass beads
◊ 8 x 3mm silver plated balls
◊ 2 jump rings
◊ 2 ear wires

Other equipment

◊ Round former
◊ Wire cutters
◊ Round-nosed pliers

1 Form a loop around a round object, choosing a suitable size for the finished loop. We used a marker pen. Wind the wire around the former. Carefully slide the wire off the former and cut the loop so that the ends overlap by about 8mm (⅜in).

2 Roll one end of the wire around your pliers. Gently turn the loop so that it is at right angles to the hoop.

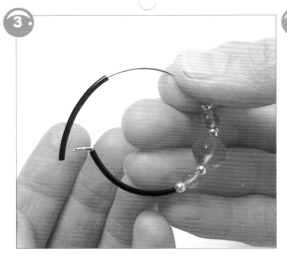

3 If you are using tubing cut it into four pieces to fit on either side of the beads; you will have to adjust the length of the tube to fit the size of the beads and the hoop. Thread on the beads. Add the second piece of tube and form another loop (see step 2).

4 Open a jump ring, slide it through the loop and close it.

5 Open the loop on an ear wire, hook it into the jump ring and close the loop.

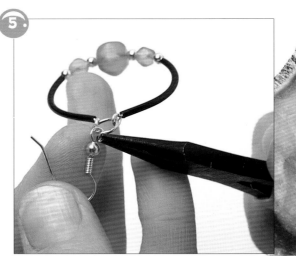

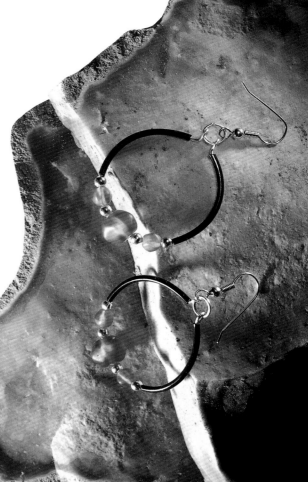

STRAIGHT EARRINGS

You will need

◊ 2 x 50mm (2in) eyepins
◊ 2 round Peruvian beads
◊ 2 Peruvian tube beads
◊ 6 x 3mm silver plate balls
◊ 2 ear wires

Other equipment

◊ Round-nosed pliers

1 Thread the beads on the eyepins, leaving a gap of about 8mm (⅜in) at the top of the pin. Rest the eyepin on your third finger and hold the beads firmly in place with your thumb and first finger. Hold the top of the eyepin with your pliers, which should be close to the beads, and bend the eyepin towards you at an angle of 45 degrees.

2 Begin to make a loop by moving the pliers to the top of the eyepin and rolling the wire of the eyepin away from you, around the top of the pliers. If you do not complete the loop in a single movement, take out the pliers, reposition them and roll the wire again.

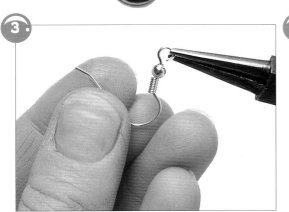

3 Take one of the ear wires and open the loop sideways.

4 Put the ear wire through the loop of your earring and close it again.

TIPS

• Remember that your first few loops are almost certain to be untidy, so have some spare eyepins and wire cutters to hand so that you can cut the loop off the drop and try again with a new pin.
• Always open the loops on eyepins or ear wires sideways.
• If the metal of an eyepin or ear wire feels weak, reject it and use another one.

BASIC TECHNIQUES

KNOTTING

If you are using precious or fragile beads you should put a knot between each bead to protect them – if a knotted necklace breaks, you will lose only one bead. When you rethread an old knotted necklace you will probably have to replace the knots so that your necklace does not become too short. You will need an additional 50 per cent more thread than the length of the finished necklace to make the knots. The Jasper Necklace on page 33 uses knots.

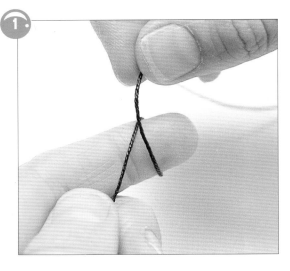

1 Start to make the knot around your finger.

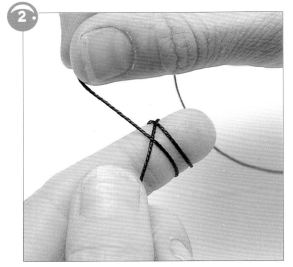

2 Make it a double knot and pull the thread through both loops.

3 Before you tighten the knot, place the needle in the knot so that you can control it.

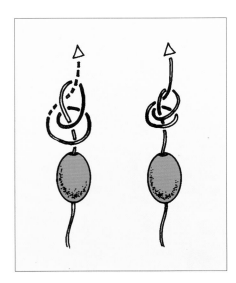

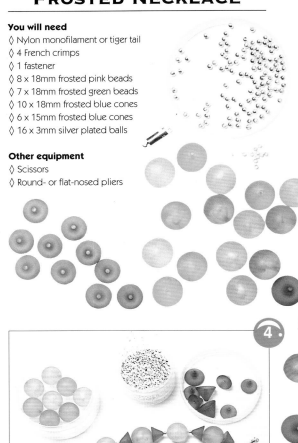

FROSTED NECKLACE

You will need
◊ Nylon monofilament or tiger tail
◊ 4 French crimps
◊ 1 fastener
◊ 8 x 18mm frosted pink beads
◊ 7 x 18mm frosted green beads
◊ 10 x 18mm frosted blue cones
◊ 6 x 15mm frosted blue cones
◊ 16 x 3mm silver plated balls

Other equipment
◊ Scissors
◊ Round- or flat-nosed pliers

4 Thread on the beads in your chosen pattern.

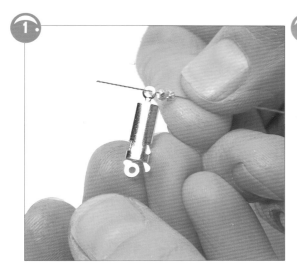

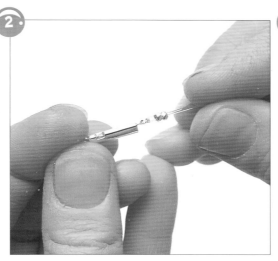

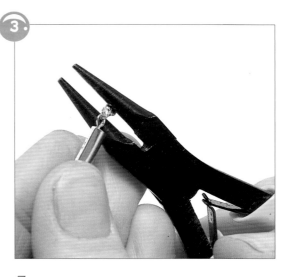

1 Cut a length of line about 55cm (21⅛in) long. Put two French crimps at one end of the line and thread through one end of the fastener.

2 Bring the line back through the crimps and make a neat loop, which should be small and tidy but not too tight against the fastener.

3 Squeeze the crimps with your pliers, making sure that they are tight but not so tight that they damage the line.

5 When you reach the other end, thread on the other two crimps. Thread the line through the fastener and loop it back through the crimps.

6 Squeeze the crimps firmly with your pliers and trim any loose ends with the scissors.

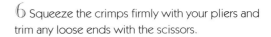

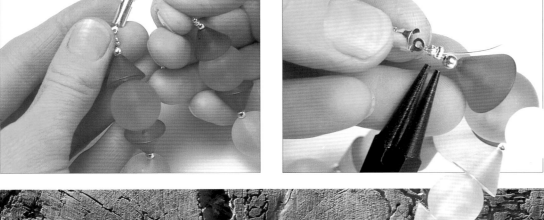

STARS AND MOONS

This delicate necklace and earring set uses crimps and gives an opportunity to practise your basic earring-making techniques and to do a little wirework.

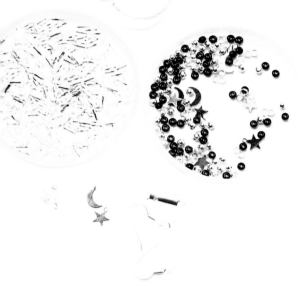

You will need

◊ 2 x 38mm (1½in) eyepins
◊ 4 x 25mm (1in) eyepins
◊ 7 stars
◊ 6 moons
◊ 30 small black glass beads
◊ 50 x 3mm silver plated balls
◊ 2 earring hoops of 0.8mm silver plated wire and jump rings or hoop findings
◊ 2 ear wires
◊ 70 silver plated 6mm Heishi tubing
◊ French crimps
◊ Fastener
◊ 7 figure-of-eight findings
◊ Tiger tail

Other equipment

◊ Round- or flat-nosed pliers
◊ Wire cutters
◊ Scissors

TIP

• Have some spare eyepins close to hand in case you overwork the metal as you open and close the loops. You will be able to feel with your pliers if the metal becomes weak.

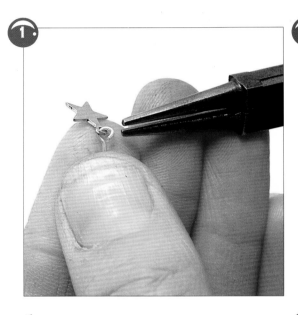

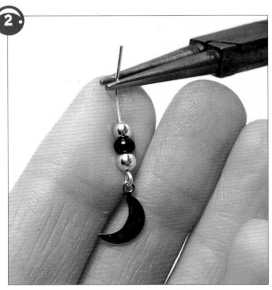

1 Beginning with the earrings, use your pliers to open the loops in the eyepins sideways. Put on the stars and moons, arranging them on the three eyepins as you wish. Carefully close the loops.

2 Thread the silver balls and black beads on the eyepins and roll the top by bending the top 8mm (⅜in) of the pin towards you to an angle of about 45 degrees. Move your pliers to the top and roll the wire around your pliers, away from you. If the loop is not quite closed, use your pliers to adjust it until there is no gap.

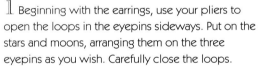

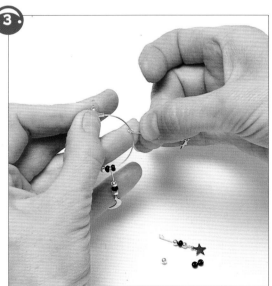

3 If you are using a ready-made hoop finding check that one side is firmly closed and open the other side, which will slide out from the hanger at the top of the hoop. Thread the beads and eyepins on to the hoop, beginning with a silver ball and a black bead. Remember that the loops in the tops of the eyepins should face in the same direction and there should be a black bead between each one.

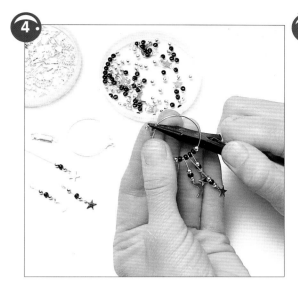

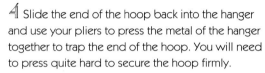

4 Slide the end of the hoop back into the hanger and use your pliers to press the metal of the hanger together to trap the end of the hoop. You will need to press quite hard to secure the hoop firmly.

5 Use your pliers to open the loop on the ear wire sideways. Insert it in the top of the hanger and close the ear wire, making sure that the point of the ear wire and rough side of the hanger face in the same direction.

6 Begin the necklace by attaching the moon and stars to the figure-of-eight findings so that they hang flat. Open one loop of the figure-of-eight sideways, put on a moon or a star and close the loop again with pliers.

7 Cut a piece of tiger tail to the length you want your necklace, adding an extra 2cm (about ¾in) at each end for the crimping. Put two crimps on one end of the tiger tail, taking care not to kink the tiger tail as you work. Thread the tiger tail through the fastener and back through the crimps. Squeeze the crimps tightly with the base of round-nosed pliers or with the tip of flat-nosed pliers. Begin to thread on the silver tubing and work to the centre of the design. Thread on the stars and moons on their findings. When you have finished the central pattern, finish off with silver tubing to match the first half.

8 Check that the pattern is symmetrical, then put on two more crimps and thread the tiger tail through the other end of the fastener. Take the tiger tail back through the crimps, check the spacing to make sure that the beads are not too tight but that there are no gaps. Squeeze the crimps and trim off the loose ends.

TIP

- If you cannot obtain hoop findings, make a hoop as shown in the techniques section (page 10).

TRIANGLES

This is a more complicated set of earrings and matching necklace, which will allow you
to develop your crimping and wirework skills.

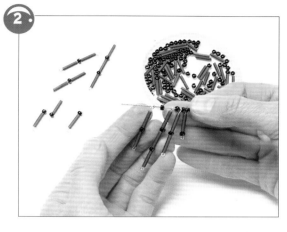

You will need

◊ 8 x 25mm (1in) eyepins
◊ 100 small glass beads, size 7/0
◊ 100 x 7mm glass bugles
◊ 17 x 50mm (2in) eyepins
◊ 2 x 5mm (¼in) jump rings
◊ 2 ear wires
◊ Tiger tail
◊ 4 French crimps
◊ Fastener

**Other
equipment**

◊ Round- or flat-nosed pliers
◊ Wire cutters
◊ Scissors

1 Begin with the hanging pieces and, with the
ready-made loop at the bottom, thread a small
bead and a bugle on the 25mm (1in) eyepins and
three bugles and two beads on three of the 50mm
(2in) eyepins. Then two bugles and one bead onto
eight of the 50mm (2in) eyepins. Shorten these
eyepins with wire cutters or by fatiguing the metal,
which you can do by gripping the wire with your
pliers about 8mm (⅜in) above the beads and
bending the wire backwards and forwards until it
snaps. Roll the tops of all the eyepins, bending the
wire close to the beads towards you and then
rolling it away from you to make a neat loop.

2 Take a 50mm (2in) eyepin and thread on it two
small beads, then the beaded hanging pieces,
threading from short to long and back again with a
small bead between each one, then two more small
beads. Roll the end of this eyepin so that the new
loop is in line with the existing one.

3 Use your pliers to open the loops on two new
eyepins sideways, hook them into the loops at each
end of the piece you have been working on and
close the loops. Alternately thread three small
beads and two bugles on each eyepin and roll
the tops.

4 Open a jump ring and put both loops through it.
Close the jump ring.

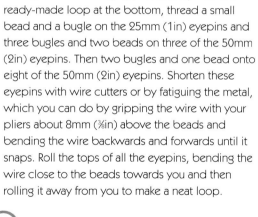

5 Open the loop on the ear wire sideways, put on the jump ring and carefully close the loop.

6 Cut a piece of tiger tail for the necklace, adding at least 2cm (about ¾in) at each end for crimping. Put two crimps on one end, thread the tiger tail through the fastener and then back through the crimps. Squeeze the crimps firmly with your pliers. Begin to thread on the bugles, with a glass bead between each one. When you get to the centre, thread on the hanging pieces you have already made. Finish the other side to match.

7 Check that your design is symmetrical. Put two crimps on the end, thread the tiger tail through the other side of the fastener and make sure that the beads are not too tight. Thread the tiger tail back through the crimps, squeeze them together and trim off the ends.

VENETIAN-STYLE GLASS NECKLACE

This dramatic necklace and glamorous matching hatpin are made from lovely Indian beads, which are made in the same way as old Venetian beads, and Thai silver beads. These are simple pieces to make but will give you some ideas for designs of your own.

You will need
◊ Tiger tail
◊ 40 tiny blue beads size 7/0
◊ 12 ornate drop beads
◊ 8 ornate round beads
◊ 4 small Thai silver beads
◊ 1 large Thai silver bead
◊ 50 x 5mm blue glass beads
◊ 50 x 6mm turquoise beads
◊ French crimps
◊ Fastener
◊ Hatpin with clutch

Other equipment
◊ Scissors
◊ Round- or flat-nosed pliers
◊ Clear, all-purpose adhesive

1 Cut a length of tiger tail, allowing an extra 3cm (1¼in) at each end. Thread on a tiny blue bead and slide it to the centre of the tiger tail. With both ends together, thread on a drop bead. Still using two threads together, thread the hanging group of beads, ending with the large Thai silver bead.

2 Separate the two threads and work on one side at a time. Thread on a tiny blue bead and continue as follows: turquoise round bead, tiny blue bead, ornate drop, 5mm blue, turquoise round bead, 5mm blue, ornate round, 5mm blue, turquoise round bead, 5mm blue bead, ornate drop (upside down), tiny blue bead, turquoise round bead, tiny blue bead, small Thai silver bead.

TIP

• Cut a good length of tiger tail but take care that it does not kink as you work.

3 This pattern is used one and a half times on each side of the necklace. Take care to push the beads down towards the centre as you thread them on. Make sure that both sides are symmetrical.

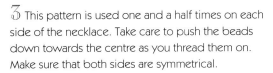

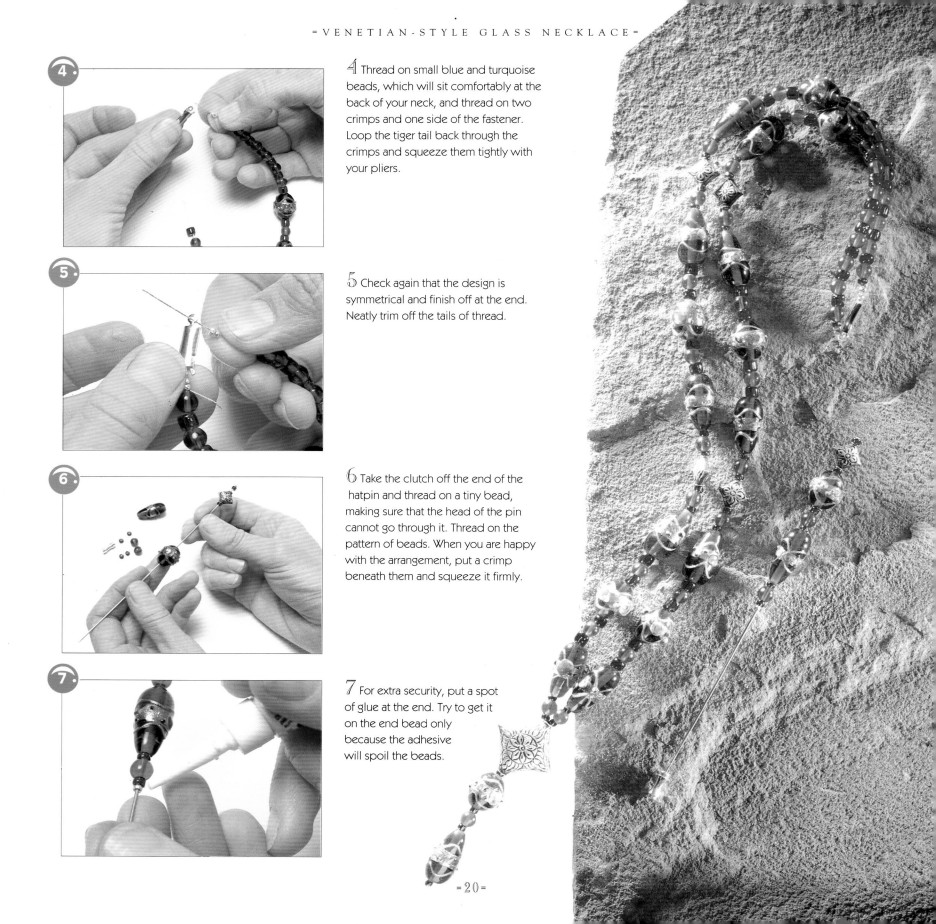

4 Thread on small blue and turquoise beads, which will sit comfortably at the back of your neck, and thread on two crimps and one side of the fastener. Loop the tiger tail back through the crimps and squeeze them tightly with your pliers.

5 Check again that the design is symmetrical and finish off at the end. Neatly trim off the tails of thread.

6 Take the clutch off the end of the hatpin and thread on a tiny bead, making sure that the head of the pin cannot go through it. Thread on the pattern of beads. When you are happy with the arrangement, put a crimp beneath them and squeeze it firmly.

7 For extra security, put a spot of glue at the end. Try to get it on the end bead only because the adhesive will spoil the beads.

A CHAIN OF FISHES

Ceramic fish and painted fish beads from Peru swim along on a chain of swivels. Simple earring-making techniques have been built up to make this chain and matching earrings.

1 Start with a fish bead, an eyepin and some tiny beads and balls. Thread on the main bead with the small beads on either side. Roll the top of the eyepin by bending the wire towards you until it is at an angle of 45 degrees. Move the pliers to the top and roll the wire around the pliers to make a neat loop.

2 Carefully open the loop to the side, insert a swivel and close the loop.

You will need
◊ 6 fish beads
◊ 25 x 50mm (2in) eyepins
◊ 70 tiny grey beads, size 8/0
◊ 70 x 3mm silver plated balls
◊ 17 x 18mm (¾in) swivels
◊ 8 striped ceramic beads
◊ 4 ceramic fish
◊ 2 ear wires
◊ Fastener or extra swivel

Other equipment
◊ Round-nosed pliers

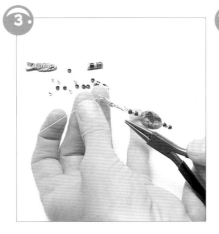

TIP

• If any of the eyepins feel weak, reject them and use a new one.

3 Add another eyepin to the swivel by opening the bottom loop of the eyepin and hooking it through the swivel. Close the loop neatly.

4 Thread a striped bead onto the eyepin with some small beads on either side and roll the top.

5 Continue to build up the chain in the same way, working alternately at each side of the first fish bead to make sure the design is symmetrical.

6 The chain is long enough to go over your head, but if you want to use a fastener, add it instead to one of the swivels between one of the fish bead and striped bead sections. Hook it between two loops in the same way as the other pieces.

7 Make the earrings in the same way as the chain, using a painted fish bead and a swivel. Open the loops of the ear wires and hang the swivels from them. Close the ear wires neatly.

DOUBLE STRIPY NECKLACE

This project contrasts decorative metallized plastic beads, striped Guatemalan beads and some pretty small glass beads.

The piece involves managing threads and using calottes.

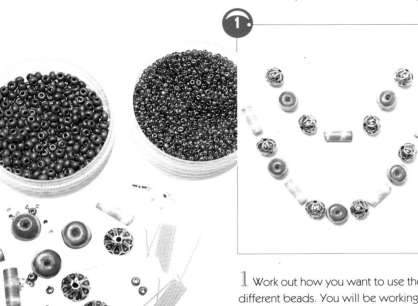

1 Work out how you want to use the different beads. You will be working from one end to the other and working the silk around the whole necklace.

2 Unwrap some silk from each card – do not unwrap too much, or the silks will become tangled – and start by threading both threads through one frosted bead. Separate the threads and thread a tiny bead onto each. Alternate frosted and tiny beads five times on each thread, then thread both silks through one frosted bead again. Separate the silks and repeat the pattern.

You will need

◊ 200 x 5mm frosted glass beads
◊ 200 tiny glass beads, size 8/0
◊ 4 striped Guatemalan tubes
◊ 2 striped round Guatemalan beads
◊ 4 metallized plastic beads
◊ 2 cards of silk with attached needles
◊ 2 calottes
◊ Fastener

Other equipment

◊ Scissors
◊ Darning needle
◊ Round- or flat-nosed pliers

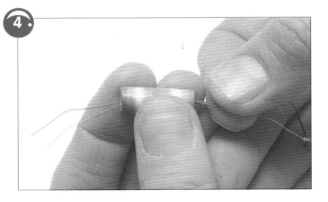

3 Each time you complete a selection of beads, unwind some of the silk and pull the threaded section of beads back towards the cards. Allow a comfortable amount of silk to work with.

4 When you have four sections of glass beads, put both threads through a frosted bead, through one of the striped tubes and through a frosted bead. Make another section and thread both silks through a metallized bead with frosted beads on each side. Thread another section, then thread the central pattern with a frosted bead between each large bead.

TIP

• If you keep moving the work back on the silk towards the cards, you will still have the needles on what is left of the thread for use another time.

= 25 =

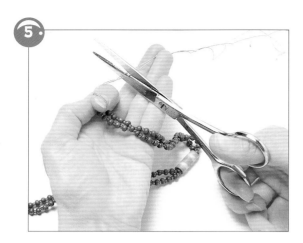

5 Keep moving the design back along the silks as you work. When you have completed the design, check that it is symmetrical and cut the threads, allowing an extra 6cm (2⅜in) at each end.

6 Tie both strands of the silk together at one end and place a thick needle in the knot. As you tighten the knot, guide it back towards the end bead so that it sits neatly against it.

7 Put a calotte over the knot and use your pliers to close the calotte, which must be secure but not so tight that it damages the silks. Repeat the knotting and fit a calotte at the other end. Trim the loose ends of the silk with sharp scissors.

8 Use pliers to open the loops at each end of a screw fastener, put the calottes on them and close the loops neatly.

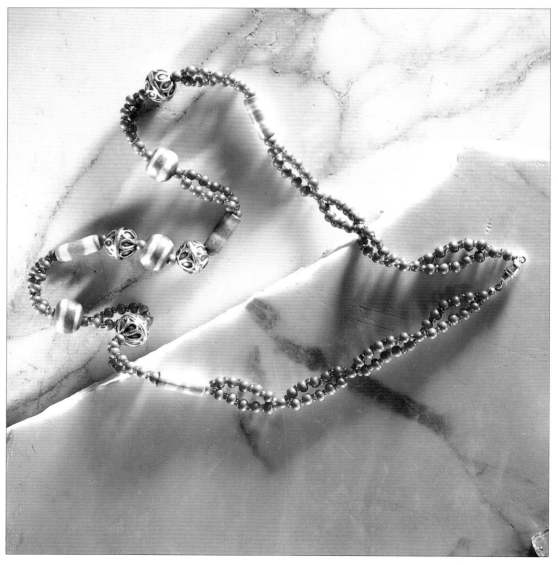

CHINA BLUE NECKLACE

───●───

This project demonstrates how very simple techniques can produce very sumptuous results. By threading a variety of Chinese porcelain beads and different glass beads and by using basic crimping techniques, you can make a really stunning necklace.

You will need

◊ Black or blue polyester thread
◊ 10 round Chinese beads
◊ 1 triangle bead
◊ 10 oblong Chinese beads
◊ 16 enamelled bead caps
◊ 8 x 8mm round beads
◊ 80 blue glass beads
◊ 100 green frosted beads
◊ 200 small black beads
◊ 20 French crimps
◊ 2 cones
◊ Fastener

Other equipment

◊ Scissors
◊ Round- or flat-nosed pliers

TIP

• Stand in front of a mirror and hold the strands in front of you so that you can check your choice of beads in the reflection.

①

1 Cut four lengths of thread, each about 50cm (20in) long, and lay them out. Thread beads on to each one at the same time, working to achieve a pleasing balance among the different strands. Aim to have the smaller beads towards the outside of the pattern and leave about 8cm (3¼in) of thread at each side of all the threads. The enamelled bead caps should be threaded either side of the plain 8mm round beads to give the extra richness.

②

2 When you are happy with the pattern of the strands, hold each strand carefully at each end to check that it hangs well. Take this opportunity to reposition any beads that do not look right. At this stage you should still have some of each of the beads left.

3 Make a small loop at one end of a strand, slide a crimp on it and squeeze the crimp with your pliers. Move the beads towards this end, make a loop, add a crimp at the other end and squeeze the crimp. Repeat with the other strands and trim off all loose ends.

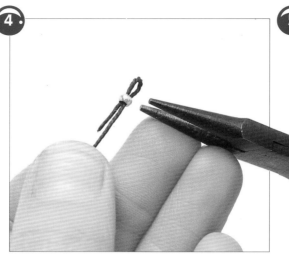

4 Cut two more lengths of thread, each about 20cm (8in) long, and make a loop at one end of each.

5 Take the short pieces of thread through the loops at the end of the beaded strands. Pass the threads back into their own end loops.

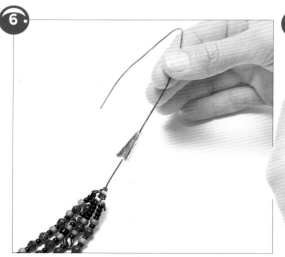

6 Thread a cone onto each short piece so that the ends of the beaded strands are neatly hidden.

7 Thread beads onto the two short ends; you can make these symmetrical or work a slightly random pattern. When you are happy with the length of the necklace, put two crimps on one end of one of the threads and take the end through a loop in the fastener and then back through the crimps.

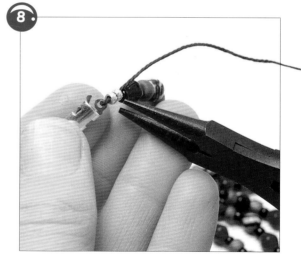

8 Squeeze the crimps with your pliers and check that they are tight. Repeat this at the other side with the other end of the fastener before trimming off all loose ends.

CLAY AND TILE BEAD NECKLACE

This necklace is more complicated to make, but if you work through the steps carefully, you will make a lovely thick cluster of rope and tassels.

You will need
◊ White polyester thread
◊ 300 white tile beads
◊ 400 tiny brown beads
◊ 1 clay ring
◊ 2 large round clay beads
◊ 10 clay discs
◊ French crimps
◊ Wire
◊ 2 bell caps
◊ Fastener

Other equipment
◊ Glue
◊ Round- or flat-nosed pliers
◊ Wire cutters
◊ Clear, all-purpose adhesive

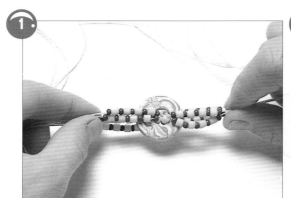

1 Cut four lengths of thread, each about 80cm (32in) long, and thread 10 white tiles and 11 small brown beads alternately on the centre of each. Thread two of these into each side of the clay ring so that four lengths emerge from both sides.

2 Put these four threads through a large clay bead on either side of the central ring.

3 Working on one side, thread on five white tiles and six small brown beads alternately on each of the threads and put all four threads through a clay disc.

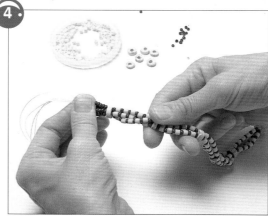

4 Work four more sections and push all the beads back towards the central ring. Pick up five small brown beads on each thread and push them back.

5 Make a small, neat loop at the end of each thread and put a crimp on it. When the loops are neat and even on each thread, squeeze the crimps.

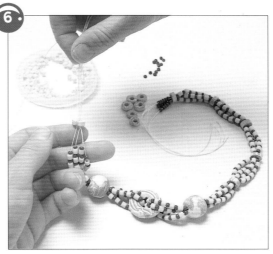

6 Repeat the pattern on the other side, making the patterns symmetrical and pushing the beads back towards the centre before crimping the loops at the ends of each thread.

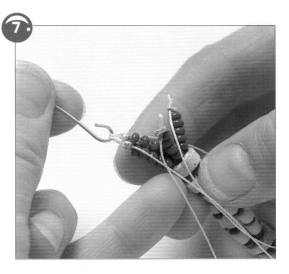

7 Use wire cutters to cut a small length of wire. Roll the wire around the round-nosed pliers to make a loop. Put the loops on the ends of the threads through this and close it neatly.

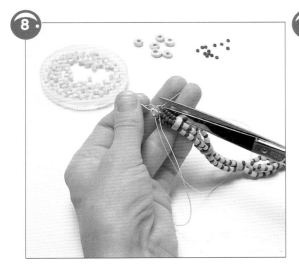

8 Trim all the ends of thread.

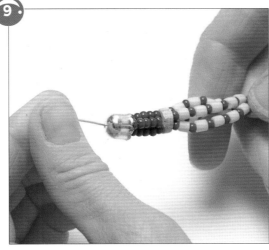

9 Put the bell cap on the wire. Clip the wire, leaving just sufficient to make a neat loop.

10 Make the loop with your pliers, open it sideways to hook on the fastener and close the loop neatly. Repeat to match at the other side.

11 Cut three pieces of thread, each about 18cm (7in) long, and make a firm knot at one end of each length, adding a spot of adhesive to the knot. Leave the glue to dry and thread on some small brown beads and white tile beads. You can make the threads the same or slightly different lengths if you prefer.

12 As each short length is half-threaded, work it through the clay ring, then add the beads to the other end of the thread.

13 Make a knot at the loose end of each length, placing a needle in the knot so that you can slide it back towards the beads. Make sure the beads are close together but not so tight that they are rigid. When you are happy with the knot, put a spot of adhesive on the knot, avoiding the beads if possible, and trim the ends of the tassels.

Monochrome Choker

Beads similar to those in the centre of this choker have been made for over a century for pilgrims to Mecca.

This project combines them with black and white beads to introduce one of the first stages of bead weaving.

1 Unwrap a reasonable amount of black silk from both cards and straighten the needles so that they are ready for use.

2 Take both threads through a white bead, separate the threads and pick up a black bead on each. Take both threads through another white bead before picking up a black bead on each thread. Repeat this pattern.

You will need
◊ 2 cards of black silk with attached needles
◊ 35 white glass beads
◊ 70 black glass beads
◊ 5 mosque beads
◊ White silk
◊ 2 black beads with large holes

Other equipment
◊ Scissors
◊ Masking tape (optional)

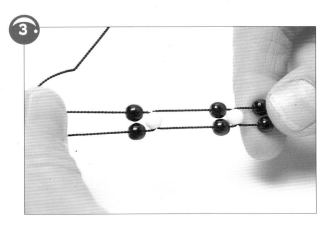

3 Keep pulling the beads back towards the cards and release more silk as you work.

4 As you reach the centre of the choker, replace alternate white beads with the mosque beads, taking the thread through from each side of the bead in the same way. Continue to pull the choker back towards the cards. You should aim to have about 30cm (12in) of thread at each end of the choker.

5 When the beads are threaded and you are sure they are firmly and correctly placed, cut a 120cm (4ft) length of white silk for each end. Using it double, tie one onto one end of the choker with the black silks.

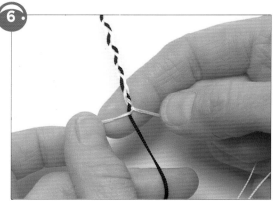

6 Working with the black threads together, plait the three double strands together. You might find it easier to plait the threads if you use masking tape to hold the choker to your working surface.

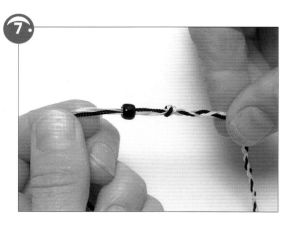

7 About 8cm (3¼in) from the end of the silk threads, knot them with a simple knot. Thread on one of the beads with a large hole.

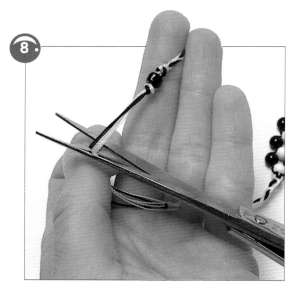

8 Make another simple knot close to this bead and trim the ends of the silks neatly. Finish the other end of the choker in the same way and wear it tied around your neck, with the ends hanging attractively down the back.

JASPER NECKLACE

These chunky semi-precious beads are knotted onto thick thread to create an ethnic look. Making this necklace will allow you to master the knotting technique that can be used with different kinds of beads to give different effects.

1 Cut a length of thread that is almost double the length that you want the necklace to be. You need extra thread to knot between the beads, plus some extra for knotting near the fastener. Make a single knot about 10cm (4in) from one end and place your needle through it. Tighten the knot but leave the needle in place.

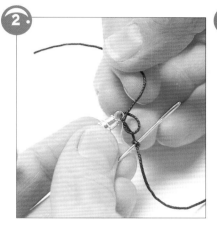

2 Put the fastener on, tying it with a single knot about 2cm (¾in) from the first knot.

3 Make a series of neat single knots to fill the gap between the two original knots. Make a loop around the main thread, bring the short end through and tighten it.

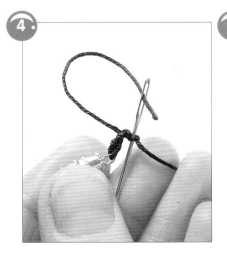

4 When you reach the first knot and needle, thread the short end through the needle and draw it through the original knot. This will make the end secure.

5 Thread on the first bead. If you can, push the short end through it to neaten the end. If you cannot, trim the short end and put a spot of adhesive on the short end to hold it. Wait until the adhesive is dry before pushing the bead against the knot.

You will need
◊ Polyester thread, silk or similar thread
◊ About 20 20mm jasper beads
◊ Fastener

Other equipment
◊ Scissors
◊ Needle
◊ Clear, all-purpose adhesive
◊ Curved, fine-pointed tweezers (optional)

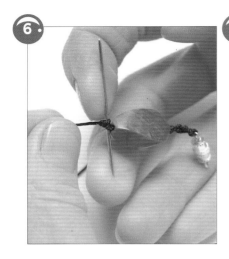

6 Make a double knot after the bead when it is in place and put the point of a needle into the knot. Use the needle to guide the knot, pulling the thread gently and carefully so that the knot lies close to the bead. Pull the thread as you remove the needle so that the knot continues to tighten against the bead.

7 Keep on adding beads, making a double knot between each one. You are certain to make some knots that do not lie as neatly against the beads as you would like, but you can unpick the knots with fine tweezers, although you must take care not to damage the thread.

8 When the necklace is the correct length, make a simple knot close to the last bead and leave a needle through it. Take the end of the thread through the fastener, again leaving a gap of about 2cm (¾in). Make single knots next to the fastener to match the first side.

9 Take the short end through the needle and draw it through the knot that is next to the last bead. When the knots are neat and tight, take the short end of thread through the last bead if you can. Alternatively, cut it neatly and add a spot of adhesive, taking care not to get glue on the beads.

AFRICAN CHOKER

This choker uses powder glass beads from Ghana and old Czech beads, which were made mainly for the African market. The project involves a macramé technique, which is an attractive and useful way to use threads to finish necklaces and chokers.

1 Cut the thread in five lengths, four about 1m (3ft 3in) long and one 50cm (20in) long. Use the four longer threads to make the central patterns.

You will need
◊ 31 powder glass beads
◊ 120 brown Czech beads
◊ 2 four-hole spacer bars
◊ 4.5m (15ft) black polyester thread

Other equipment
◊ Scissors
◊ Needle
◊ Clear, all-purpose adhesive

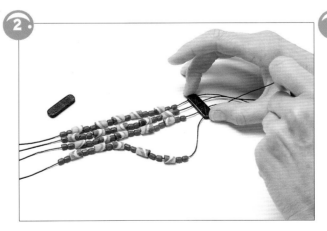

2 Thread a spacer bar on each side, then continue to pick up the beads on the four threads in pattern.

3 Use all the beads but one, which is used as a fastener, and finish off by working the four threads through a powder glass bead at each end. Loosely knot one side and trim the ends level but do not cut them short.

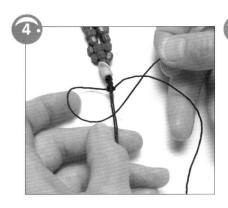

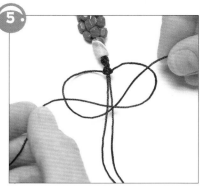

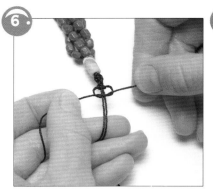

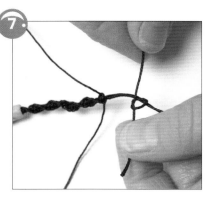

4 Make a macramé braid with the lengths of thread by keeping two threads straight in the centre and by bringing the left-hand thread under these centre threads and over the right-hand thread.

5 Take the right-hand thread over the centre threads and under the original left-hand thread.

6 Pull the ends evenly from both sides and, at the same time, pull down the centre threads to create a firm, even braid. Continue to braid the threads in this way until the choker is about 3cm (1¼in) shorter than the length you want.

7 Attach the short length of thread cut in step 1 to the centre threads.

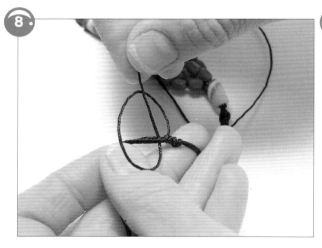

8 Use the thread to bind the centre threads to form a button loop. Take the thread over the centre threads, bring it back through its own loop and pull tightly. Continue until you have bound 2cm (¾in) of the centre threads.

9 Form the bound length into a loop and arrange all the loose ends so that they lie towards the choker. There should be a gap between the button loop and the macramé work. Return to the macramé threads and continue to work over all the loose ends by the original braiding method (steps 4, 5 and 6). Pull the threads tight as you work towards the button loop to keep the braid even and secure.

10 Check that the powder glass bead will go sideways through the loop, and pull the braid tight. Trim all loose ends close to the braid.

11 Thread the macramé ends on a needle and weave them into the braid to finish securely.

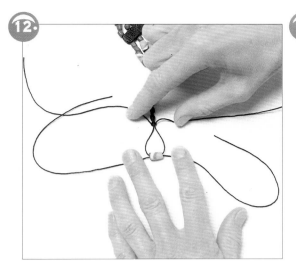

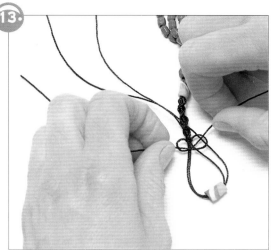

12 Undo the loose knot at the other end and push all the beads towards the other end before you start to make a braid. Use the macramé technique with the four lengths of thread, stopping about 2cm (¾in) from the finished length. Pick up the powder glass bead by threading the two central threads through the bead from opposite sides.

13 Turn these ends back towards the choker and continue with the macramé technique working firmly over these ends. When you reach the powder glass bead, pull the threads tightly together.

14 Finish off in the same way as at the other end, trimming the loose ends neatly and running the working threads back through the braid with a needle.

SPECIAL BEADS AND LEATHER

This is a good way of using "collectable" beads – some beads you might have picked up when you were on holiday abroad, for example, or from an antique shop or bead fair. If you cannot find beads exactly like the ones listed here, look out for something similar.

You will need
◊ 1 Pumtek bead from Mizoram
◊ 2 Venetian millefiori beads
◊ 2 old Turkish beads
◊ 2 brass beads from Mali
◊ 6 Indian matt glass beads
◊ Leather thonging
◊ Leather crimps
◊ 1.2mm silver plated wire

Other equipment
◊ Round-nosed pliers
◊ Wire cutters
◊ File

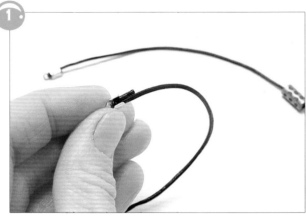

1 Arrange the beads on a length of thonging. Fold one end, and put the leather in a leather crimp. If you are using fairly thick leather, you will not need to fold it.

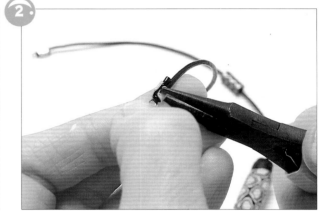

2 Use pliers to press down one side of the crimp. Then press down the other side over the first so that the leather is held firmly in the crimp.

3 If you cannot buy a hook for the crimps, make one by cutting about 3cm (1¼in) of wire.

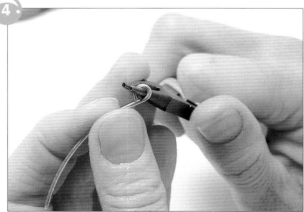

4 Hold the end of the wire with your pliers and use your thumb and first finger to roll the wire into a small loop.

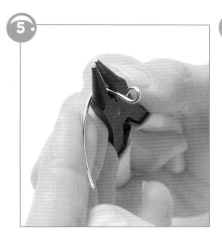

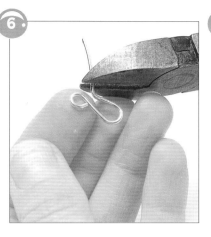

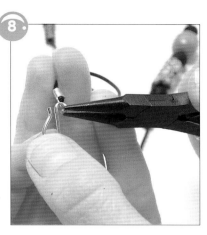

5 Use the curve in the wire and bend it around the wider part of the pliers.

6 When you have made a neat hook, bend the point a little and clip the remaining wire with wire cutters.

7 File the end smooth.

8 Open the loop on the hook sideways and insert one of the leather crimps. Close the loop. The hook will go through the leather crimp on the other end when you wear the necklace.

LAPIS AND SILVER NECKLACE

This is a stylized, somewhat abstract piece, which will develop your wire working skills and encourage you to use more tools.

You will need
◊ 6 coral glass beads
◊ 6 black glass beads
◊ 6 old silver beads
◊ 1 antique spotted bead
◊ 1 large lapis bead
◊ 4 lapis shapes
◊ 0.8mm silver plated wire
◊ 1.2mm silver plated wire
◊ Leather thonging
◊ Leather crimps

Other equipment
◊ Round-nosed pliers
◊ Wire cutters
◊ File
◊ Hammer

TIP

• Practise bending the wire and try hammering pieces on different surfaces before you start work on this project.

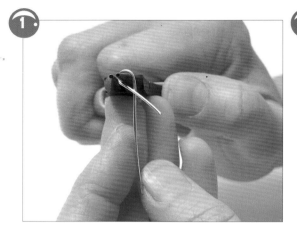

1 Wire the lapis shapes so that they will hang from the necklace. Some of the shapes that are available have holes running from top to bottom, and if you have this kind, cut a piece of 0.8mm wire and make a loop with a long end.

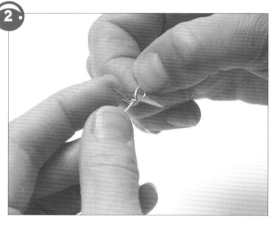

2 Use your fingers to wrap this end around the bottom of the loop.

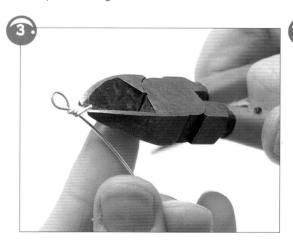

3 Make some neat coils beneath the loop, clip the end of the wire and use pliers to flatten the end of the wire under the bottom of the coils.

4 Pick up the lapis, trim the wire and use pliers to make a neat loop under the shape to hold it securely.

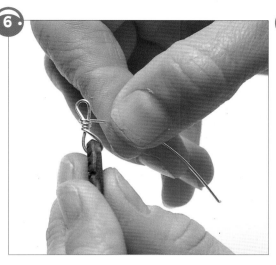

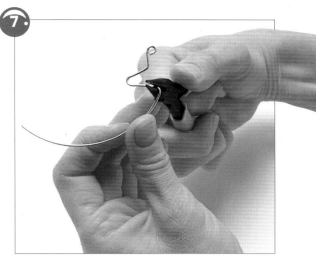

5 If the lapis shapes you have are those with a hole running from side to side, make a loop in the wire and thread it through the shape, curving the wire as you do so. Leave a gap between the loop and the lapis shape.

6 Use your finger and thumb to bend the wire firmly around the base of the loop a few times. Clip off the end of the wire and use pliers to flatten it under the coils.

7 Make the abstract wire pieces from pieces of thicker gauge wire about 20cm (8in) long. Roll the bottom end of the wire then form it into interesting shapes by curving it from side to side against your pliers.

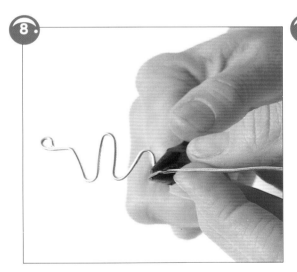

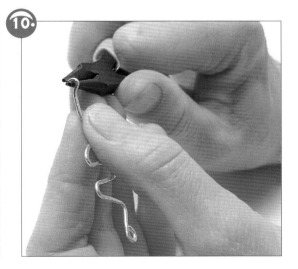

8 Continue to work until you are happy with the zigzag shape. You will need three of these shapes in all, but they need not be identical.

9 To make the necklace even more interesting, you can hammer the silver wire flat. This roughens the surface and allows you to glimpse the brass beneath the silver plating.

10 Roll the tops of the finished zigzag shapes so that they can be threaded.

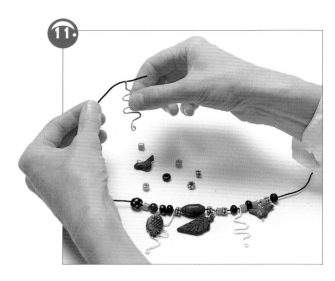

11 Thread the pieces onto the leather. These pieces look most effective if the arrangement is asymmetric.

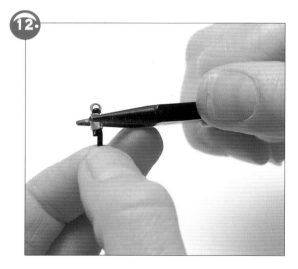

12 Put leather crimps on the ends and make a hook to fasten the necklace as described in steps 3–8 of the previous project.

SPRUNG WIRE BRACELET

This and the following project illustrate two different ideas for bracelets.

Sprung wire is easy to use, but you do need strong hands.

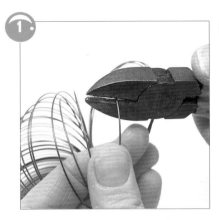

1 You can sometimes buy cut lengths of sprung wire or you can cut the necessary amount from a longer roll. You will need to press hard to do this.

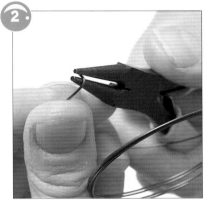

2 Use pliers to roll a loop at one end. This is quite hard to do, and you should keep moving your wire and making little turns while you hold the wire with your other hand.

3 Thread on the beads. The pattern can be random, but distribute the larger beads evenly among the smaller ones. You will need to unroll the wire from time to time so that the beads can slide down.

You will need
◊ 3 loops of sprung wire, approximately 60cm (24in)
◊ 6 small Peruvian beads
◊ 33 frosted green beads
◊ 15 turquoise and green round glass beads
◊ 65 tiny black glass beads

Other equipment
◊ Wire cutters
◊ Strong round-nosed pliers

4 Leave about 1cm (⅛in) at the end of the wire and roll the end with your pliers.

TWO-STRAND BRACELET

Although it requires patience to make, the finished bracelet is extremely pretty.

You will need

◊ Tiger tail or nylon monofilament
◊ French crimps
◊ 50 pink glass beads
◊ 50 tiny grey glass beads
◊ 6 grey faceted beads
◊ 2 two-hole spacer bars
◊ 2 split rings or jump rings
◊ Fastener

Other equipment

◊ Scissors
◊ Round- or flat-nosed pliers

1 Cut two lengths of tiger tail or monofilament to fit around your wrist, but be generous or the work will become fiddly and time consuming. Allow an extra 6cm (2⅜in) on each strand. Put two crimps near the end of one strand and loop the tiger tail back through them. Squeeze the crimps with your pliers. Pick up the first beads and take the thread through the top of the spacer bar.

2 Continue working on this strand, picking up the beads in pattern for the central section before threading on the second spacer bar. When the strand is symmetrical, put on two more crimps, make another neat loop to match the first and squeeze the crimps firmly.

3 Make another matching loop on the second strand and repeat the pattern of beads, threading through the lower hole in the spacer bars in the appropriate places.

4 Carefully open a jump ring or split ring and thread on both loops and a fastener. Repeat this at the other end.

TIP

• Split rings will make the bracelet stronger than jump rings, but they are more difficult to use. Try working a strong needle between the rings to hold them open.

LOOM-MADE BRACELET

This is an easy project to work on a beading loom. When you have mastered this bracelet
you will be ready to try some more ambitious pieces.

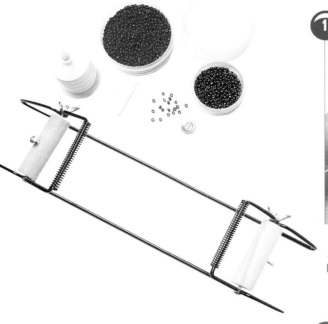

You will need
◊ 160 white rocailles, size 8/0
◊ 60 black rocailles, size 8/0
◊ 30 blue rocailles, size 8/0
◊ White polyester loom thread
◊ Button

**Other
equipment**
◊ Loom
◊ Scissors

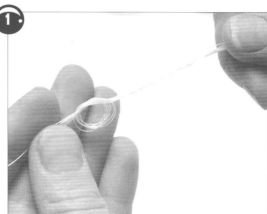

1 Cut seven warp threads, each 80cm (about 32in) long, and knot them together at one end.

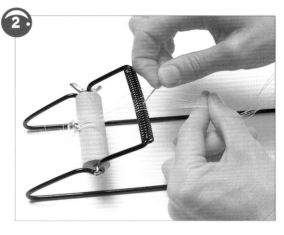

2 Tighten the bars on the loom, then hook the warp threads on one end of it and bring them over the bar. Use a needle to separate the threads until they lie side by side in the grooves of the loom.

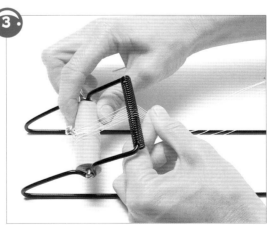

3 Turn the roller a few times to make sure that the warp threads are taut.

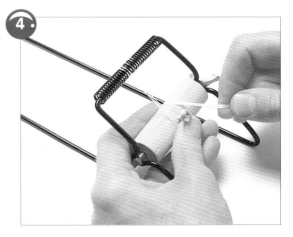

4 Take the threads down the loom and separate them over the opposite grooves at the other end. Secure the warp threads around this roller, keeping the threads as taut as you can.

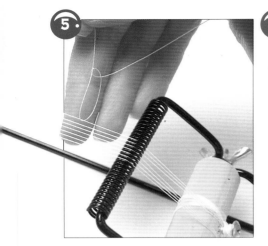

5 Cut a beading thread about 1.5m (5ft) long and tie it to an outside warp thread. Thread it on a needle.

6 Keeping the beading thread below the warp threads, position two rocailles in the centre two spaces. Bring up your needle before the two outside warp threads.

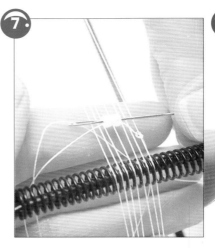

7 Thread the needle back through the two rocailles, working over the warp threads. Repeat this step with two beads four more times and then take the beading thread down between the first and second warp threads. Use four rocailles for two rows.

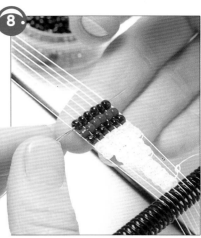

8 Start to work over the full width of the warp threads so that six rocailles fit into the spaces. Work the pattern with black and blue rocailles.

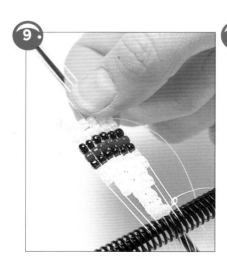

9 As you work along the loom, keep moving the rocailles back against the previous row to keep the work firm.

10 When you have completed the pattern and reduced the number of rocailles at the other end of the bracelet, loosen the rollers at both ends and take the bracelet off the loom.

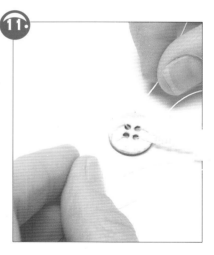

11 Put the button on one end by threading four of the warp threads through the buttonholes, knotting them neatly behind and working the warp threads back into the bracelet.

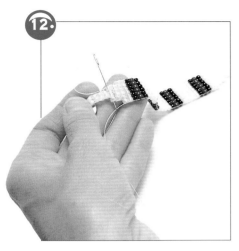

12 Work the other warp threads at this end back into the rocailles and trim them neatly once they are securely finished off.

13 At the other end, use a needle to thread about eight additional rocailles (depending on the size of the button) onto each of the centre two warp threads.

14 Work each thread back down the opposite row of rocailles to form a loop with the two threads running through it in opposite directions. Tighten the threads and use a needle to weave the ends back into the bracelet. Finish this end by weaving the warp threads back into the bracelet and trimming off the loose ends once they are securely finished off.

SUPPLIERS

UK

Bead Shop
43 Neal Street
Covent Garden
London WC2H 9PJ

Hobby Horse
15–17 Langton Street
London SW10 0JL

London Bead Company
25 Chalk Farm Road
London NW1 8AG

Beads
259 Portobello Road
London W11 1LR

Rocking Rabbit Trading Company
Market Street
Newmarket
Suffolk CB8 8EE

MAIL ORDER ONLY

Bojangles
Old Cottage
Appleton
Oxon OX13 5JH

Ahenzi
91 High Street
Winslow
Bucks MK18 3DG

USA

Beadworks
For catalogue:
139 Washington Street
Norwalk
CT 06854

Peruvian Bead Company
1601 Callens Road
Ventura
CA 93003

AUSTRALIA

Creative Bead Imports
255 South Terrace
South Fremantle
Western Australia

WORKSHOPS WITH SARA WITHERS

Available through
Oxford Arts & Crafts
Gable End
Hatford
Near Faringdon
Oxon SN7 8JF

Bead Society of Great Britain
Carole Morris
1 Casburn Lane
Burwell
Cambs CB5 0ED